Becoming a Digital Baller
Baller
The Playbook

Connor Wright

This book is dedicated to Larry Gelwix who taught me the concept of FIO.
FIO has helped me in every aspect of life.

CONTENTS

ACKNOWLEDGMENTS

Thank you to all those who helped me in the process of writing this book.

A huge thank you to one of my greatest mentors, Bryan Hatch. You gave me my big break and believed in me when I was just getting started. You set me down this path and I will always be grateful.

Chapter 1

Getting started in Digital Marketing

So you've started your business. Bravely stepped out into the world of entrepreneurship. You have an amazing product or service that you have a passion for and believe in. Maybe you've been planning this for a while and have planned every step of the way. You know how you're going to make this work from start to finish. Or maybe you're like many people who start their business and just go with it.

You're trying to get out of the 9 to 5 prison/monotony and get what most people want: freedom. If you've been trying to make this work for a while, you've already learned that customers don't just line up begging you to take their money. You've realized you're spending most of your time trying to find customers rather than actually doing what you set out to do.

It's frustrating, especially if you see others being successful, making money, going on amazing vacations, and buying fancy cars and big houses. So what do you do?

You've probably asked all of your friends for referrals. Maybe you've joined masterminds or groups to network with others, or maybe you've read blogs and watched videos teaching about business and entrepreneurship. After doing all of this you've probably come to the conclusion that you need to start marketing your business.

It's simple right? Just do marketing. But how? Where do you start?

How about the basics?

There are two ways a business owner can approach marketing. First, hire a marketing agency or marketing employee. You would basically put your trust in someone else to take care of it for you. Second, do it yourself. Now if you have a business with just you and/or a partner, you probably have thousands of dollars to spend on hiring out a marketing team, right? Probably not.

You might have just enough to pay for the ads but don't forget you need to pay the marketing firm for their labor also. It isn't cheap. Hiring an employee is just as expensive and more stressful. So what do you do?

Do it yourself

All the experts are saying you need to get into social media and make a Facebook or Instagram page. So you make one. Then you invite all of your friends to like it. You get a handful of likes. So you start posting about your business.

After you make 3 or 4 posts and see no results, you think to yourself, "This whole social media thing is a joke." Then you give up on it and never post again.

Maybe you're different from most people. You buckle down and stick with it, trusting what all the experts say and trying to learn everything you can. You go to webinars and download free eBooks about Facebook marketing and finding success in the digital world. Then you start purchasing courses and trainings that will teach you everything you need to know. If you're lucky, after a while you'll start seeing some success, but only after spending a lot of time and money.

The problem is the gurus and experts make it seem like you will start making 6 or 7 figures by next week if you do this one strategy. Once they are about to teach you the good stuff, they drop the bomb that in order to get their secret you have to pay thousands of dollars for their help. Now you're stuck and don't know what to do.

Most business owners have this kind of story or one very similar. They experience frustration, anxiety, stress, and depression when it all doesn't work quickly. That is one of the reasons businesses fail within the first year of starting. It's not that they didn't work hard or have a can-do attitude, they just didn't know how to do marketing.

Unfortunately, many of these failed businesses have amazing products or services! They are good people trying to make a difference in the world. They are trying to build a better life for themselves and their families. They have dreams of freedom, vacations, new toys, or wealth. They are passionate about what they sell. If only others could see how their product or service could change lives, people would be lining up at the door!

Marketing is helping people see the value of your product and understand your business's mission statement. When you know how to do marketing correctly, you find your ideal customer and present your product in a way that helps them decide to buy.

Every business needs marketing of some kind, but there is so much to learn. There are thousands if not millions of guides, tips, courses, books, and blogs - all telling you what to do. Additionally, there are hundreds of new marketing software popping up every day that claim they can "do it all".

You have two options to choose from.

Choice 1: Give up. Quit and go back to the 9 to 5. It's too hard, and you take the easy road.

Choice 2: Learn how to be a marketer.

Before you start jumping into every webinar and training out there to learn marketing you need to start at the beginning. You need to learn marketing fundamentals. You need to learn the basics.

You see, every business owner needs to be a marketer. Even if you have a budget to pay someone else to do it, you still need to know what strategy the marketer is using, where you're getting the best results, and what is and isn't working. If you don't have an understanding of marketing you'll be left trusting someone else with your business.

Hiring someone else

If you don't know marketing, you will never be happy with the results. The reason is marketing results aren't always directly reflected in instant dollars. Results can be slow, but if you know what's going on you won't panic and make poor decisions.

One of those poor decisions could be hiring a marketing firm that doesn't know what it's doing. You need to understand marketing so you can see past the bull s***. Anyone who has run ads on Facebook can say he/she is a Facebook marketer, but that doesn't mean he or she is any good. It takes less than 5 minutes to throw a Facebook ad together. A child could do it after watching one YouTube video.

So if you're a personal trainer you also need to be a personal trainer/marketer. If you're an insurance agent you also need to be an insurance agent/marketer. If you're a hairstylist you also need to be a hairstylist/marketer. You can't just focus on being a life coach; you also need to focus on marketing as a life coach. The world's best life coach who can't do marketing will have fewer clients than an average life coach who is amazing at marketing.

Fundamentals

I have been doing digital marketing for a while now. I actually majored in social media marketing, and yes, you can get a degree in that now. I've been a Director of Marketing for a multimillion-dollar tech company. I've also done digital marketing and consulting for multiple businesses: helping them create and implement marketing strategies that saw amazing results.

I tell you this not to brag, but because I am doing a marketing fundamental right now. You've got to practice what you preach right? I want you to know that I am an authority on the subject of digital marketing. I'll go over more of why I did this in the chapter 6.

In my time doing marketing and training others, I've seen that marketers today are getting further and further away from basic marketing principles and best practices. With the amount of marketing software and tools available, the marketing community is starting to rely too much on the tools and less on the skills it takes to make those tools effective. Software doesn't make you better at marketing if you are not already practicing basic fundamentals.

Let me give you a sports analogy. In major league baseball, you have some hitters that crush home runs over 400 feet. Why are they so good? Do they just practice hitting home runs? No. They hit off a tee. That's right. Remember playing t-ball as a kid? The pros are still doing that. But why?

When hitting off a tee, they build muscle memory of the perfect swing. When they have this muscle memory perfected, they can do the exact same perfect swing every time. So whether they have a 60 mile per hour fastball or a 99 mile per hour fastball come in, they do the exact same perfect swing.

On the tee, they are making sure their hips rotate at the right time, making sure they don't over rotate their hands, and keeping their chin in and their eye on the ball. These are basic fundamentals that help them have the perfect swing over and over.

They become so disciplined that even when the pitcher decides to throw a curveball, they're ready. It doesn't mean they are going to hit a homerun every time. If a pro baseball player is hitting only 3 out of 10 pitches he is considered amazing. That's only a 30% success rate! Makes you wish your parents were ok with a 30% on your high school tests, right?

With both baseball and marketing, there are fundamentals. If you can gain a basic understanding of the fundamentals, you can go into any type of marketing or marketing platform and find success. Whether it is email, social media, SMS, BOTS, PPC, blogs, or SEO, by learning and perfecting the fundamentals, you can achieve success.

If you have accomplished the fundamentals, you can test to see if the platform you are using is right for your business. Once you know it's the right one for you, and you start to see some success, then invest more time into mastering it. Not every business needs to be using Google AdWords (PPC) as well as Facebook ads. You don't need to be using EVERYTHING… yet.

The Secret

Now here is a secret most marketers don't want to admit. I'm letting you in on this secret so you aren't surprised when you get stuck or aren't seeing instant success. Marketing is really just trial and error, and marketers don't really always know what will work.

There are effective high-level strategies that you can use across most businesses to see great results. There are many marketers that have amazing case studies or have done amazing things and made businesses a lot of money. That doesn't mean those strategies and marketers will work every time, on every marketing platform, on every budget, and for every business.

If you've been on social media then you've probably seen advertisements on how to "run the perfect webinar" or "5 Facebook™ hacks that get you massive ROI" or "learn all the secrets the top marketers won't tell you". Now in the chapter 4 and 5, I'll go over exactly what they are doing (you'll never be on social media the same way again… #sorrynotsorry).

Before you jump into their "free" training that will make you millions, let me explain what it's like being a marketer. This is a step by step process that all marketers use after they have learned the fundamentals:

Step 1: Try an advertisement.

Step 2: Look at the data (by the end of this book you will understand the basics of looking at and understanding the data).

Step 3: Make adjustments (when you understand what the data is telling you then you will know where and why to make adjustments).

Step 4: Repeat steps 1-3.

F.I.O.

Yes, marketing in its most basic form is just testing ads and promotions to see what works. It's all experimenting and seeing what speaks to your audience and brings them in. That's why some strategies work to market personal trainers but don't work to promote software companies. Different strategies for different audiences. What does work across every industry are the marketing fundamentals.

So those "free" trainings that you've been watching are great if you already are seeing results from your marketing efforts and you're ready for the next level. These trainings can offer great value, but if you aren't doing the marketing fundamentals you will create bad habits and never be as effective as you could be. You need to crawl before you walk.

Hopefully, by now you are convinced you need to figure out the fundamentals of marketing. At least you should see the value in having a basic understanding of marketing. Don't you want the best skill in the world when it comes to marketing? I'm about to give you gold, so ingrain this into your mind.

Before your mind starts racing, know this skill will take time to develop and master.

This skill is what I call F.I.O. Figure It Out. When something is not working you have to figure it out. Remember Steps 1-4 that were just discussed? That is the step by step formula to F.I.O. The hard truth of marketing is it takes time and money trying to make things work; figure it out.

Now don't get discouraged. That is why I wrote this book. Anyone who wants to be a marketer and grow their business can. If you understand the fundamentals you won't waste the time and money most business owners do running around trying to "find the secret". The fundamentals get you ahead of the game. Once you understand the fundamentals, the process of F.I.O. will speed up. You'll know where to start and skip basic mistakes most marketers make.

Are you ready? The next few chapters will dive into marketing fundamentals. After that, I'll get into specific tools and marketing platforms. I ask that you don't jump around in the book, even if you feel you need more help in certain places right now. I ask that of you because everything is going to build on itself. You'll miss key pieces of information that will help in other areas if you jump around. Some of the fundamentals in one chapter are important for other chapters as well.

Let's get started on making you a [insert your business] Marketer.

Chapter 2

Understanding your customers and your business

There are three levels of marketing. The first is the 1000-foot view. This is when you hear people say things like, "In order to have a business you need a product." This level has very generic answers to everything. This is the least important but most common advice given. You don't need this kind of information because it is so obvious. Yet people eat it up when super successful people give it.

I was at an event where the speaker said, "In order to be successful with an online business your website needs to look nice." I thought to myself, "Duh!" So with this book, I promise to stay away from this style of advice and stick to teaching you things that you can actually apply right now.

The next level is the 500-foot view. This is a more valuable view and where most of the marketing fundamentals are. You need to gain the understanding of this level before trying all of the secret formulas and tricks you see advertised. Most of this book will be devoted to this level while scratching the surface of the next level.

The third level is the ground level. It has more in-depth strategies, tips, hacks, and tricks. It includes tactics specifically for your business or industry. This is like when a consultant comes in and dives deep into your business, giving you things to change and implement. This is my favorite level.

The reason I love this level is because I know the fundamentals. I have mastered the 500-foot view and need to dive even deeper. This level is applicable to those who are already having success in digital marketing and trying to get better. This is where you really start to FIO.

This is where case studies live. Stats and statistics really pay off here. But for a new marketer, these things can be distracting and not applicable. For example, who cares which call to action button color on a landing page works best if you have forgotten to put a call to action button on your landing page! (I have actually seen this happen).

Now I will dive into the ground level occasionally in this book, but only when it is necessary or valuable. Remember we need to hit off the baseball tee first before we start hitting home runs.

Rookie Mistake

When you start marketing for the first time, what is the first thing you need to figure out? You must first know to whom you are selling. The answer is never "everybody". This is really important to understand.

You need to know where you are going before you start down a path; otherwise, you will get lost quickly. There are so many things trying to pull your attention so it's easy to get distracted. Before trying to make a Facebook page or website, you need to first identify who you are selling to.

My next statement may be obvious to some, but I wouldn't try and sell makeup to men. Even though men occasionally buy makeup, it doesn't mean I want to spend money getting my ads in front of them. It will cost more time and money than it is worth to try and get them to buy, compared to women who actually use the product.

This is marketing 101. You need to focus on your ideal client. Don't waste time on the wrong type of people.

Let me give you an example. When I meet a business owner who wants to start digital marketing, this is the conversation I usually have. This exact conversation is a word for word discussion with the owner of a tech company for which I had become the Director of Marketing.

Me: "Do you know who your ideal client is?"

Him: "Business owners."

Me: "Ok, what kind of business owners?"

Him: "All business owners. Anyone can use our software."

Me: "What kind of businesses use the software the most?"

Him: "Insurance agents, MLM people, supplementing companies, sales reps, tire shops, realtors, and plasma centers."

Me: "I need more details so I can write ads to those people."

Him: "Just write ads for everyone."

This was one of the most frustrating conversations of my career. Unfortunately, it's very common. You see, the more generalized your client base is, the harder it will be for you. How are you or anyone else supposed to find and reach your ideal customer if you don't know who you are looking for? If you don't know, you might end up trying to sell binoculars to a blind person.

Identify your potential customers

You need to identify exactly WHO is your client. You can do this by figuring out WHAT makes your client who they are and WHY your client should buy or has bought from you. Identifying your client is one of the most important steps in marketing.

In order to correctly identify your client, you need to first look at the demographics. The demographics are the physical features of your customers. To get started you need to start asking yourself some questions. Be specific.

WHO: Men or Women? Age range? Married? Have kids? How many kids? Ethnicity? Where do they live? Homeowner or renter? Income level? What kind of car do they drive? What level of education do they have?

WHAT: What do they spend their money on? Are they early adopters of new trends or technology? What social media platforms do they use? Do they shop at Walmart or Amazon? What religion do they practice? What celebrities do they like? What shows do they watch? What are their favorite restaurants? Do they eat fast food or dine in? What are their hobbies and interests?

These are just a few of the questions you can ask yourself when trying to determine your ideal client. My goal when analyzing demographics of clients is to apply at least 10 qualifiers for each question of the WHO and the WHAT. It can take time, so be patient. Write all your questions down before answering any of them. This will help you get on a roll brainstorming your list of questions.

If you sell products to businesses (B2B), then do essentially the same thing, but ask slightly different questions. What is the size of the company? What is their revenue? Are they online or brick and mortar? How much do they spend on marketing? What software do they use? How long have they been in business? Who are the decision makers?

A great way to figure out these types of things is by using surveys. You should be trying to get every single customer to fill out a survey. At the end of every purchase, ask them to fill out a quick survey. Add some incentive like a gift or future discount to make sure you get as many completed as you can.

You may not have had enough customers to really know any of these things and that's ok. If you don't have enough, or if you don't have any customers, you need to create a customer persona. A customer persona is where you simply create your ideal customer on paper by asking some questions. Who would you like your customer to be? Who would benefit the most from your product? Now, this is pretty basic, but it gets you started in the right direction.

If you know who your customer is, then when you start writing ads you will be able to connect with them more effectively. For example, let's imagine I am a personal trainer and the following are some of my clients' demographics:

- Mostly male clients
- They have a hard time losing stubborn fat
- Many are preparing for their first bodybuilding competition
- Then need to have a higher income (because my prices are higher)

A great ad would look like:

Hey guys!
Are you trying to get ready for your first show?
Not sure what you need to do to lose the last bit of stubborn fat?
Watch this short video on the number one way to burn fat!

Notice how I am being very specific with the ad? You want it so specific that if someone sees the ad, in their mind they raise their hand saying, "That's me! I need _____!"

A terrible ad would look like:

Trying to lose weight? Click here to learn more!

Who is going to click on the ad? ANYONE who wants to lose weight. You might be getting 400-pound people who aren't your specialty. They may not be able to pay your prices, and you will be spending a lot of time and money on the wrong type of client.

Same goes for any business you are trying to sell your product to. If you have a high-priced product and your ideal client is for enterprise business with 50-100 employees, you want to get in front of those kinds of businesses. A small 1-2 person business won't be able to afford what you sell, so you'll be wasting time and money with the wrong business.

Their Problem

This was the problem with the tech company I mentioned earlier. They had not identified their client, and instead were targeting everyone. The software company I was marketing for sold a marketing software based around texting. It was very effective and very simple. As most marketing software goes, it was basic.

It was originally designed for insurance agents who didn't have any kind of marketing software already in use. The ideal client persona was pretty specific. It was best for insurance agents who were solo or had a partner. The agents needed to already have a client base of 500-4000 and the agents needed to have their clients' phone numbers to really be the most effective.

Several other businesses had heard about the marketing software from friends and got it for themselves, even though they weren't insurance agents. We found that many businesses could use it and be successful because it was simple to use and applied to a range of clients. That can be the case with any business; the ideal client will not be the only ones to buy. Just like occasionally a man will buy a dress for his wife. However, that doesn't mean you should market dresses to men.

People say never turn business away and that's true, but it can make marketing much more difficult. If you don't know who you need to talk to you won't know what to say. So with the tech company, when they wanted me to go promote the software to all types of businesses the results were not pretty.

I tried to write ads that appealed to any type of business, but then we had a problem with the leads I generated. They didn't need the software. They needed things more advanced or they only had 20 clients so the software didn't help them. My boss then would get frustrated wanting "better" leads.

When we started writing ads for the right kind of businesses the difference was night and day. Our WHO persona fit Insurance Agents as I described earlier. After writing ads for that kind of agent they started opting in to learn more. They saw the value of the software for their businesses and signed up because it filled their needs. Things turned around, all because we knew WHO our ideal customer was and WHAT made them.

Now the Who and the What are very similar, but the Why is more complex. Why do they buy from you? What connects them to your business and brand? Apple makes computers and phones but so does a number of other businesses. But why do people time and time again wait outside the doors whenever Apple releases the next iPhone?

The reason is that people connect with Apple. People connect to Apple's why? So what is your why? Why do you as a business do what you do? What is your mission statement? What drives you, besides making money? This is a fundamental that businesses forget.

You need to connect with people. You do that by showing them your why. You need to show them what problem you solve and how it will help them.

What will their experience be? In the next chapter, we'll go over the fundamentals to help you do this.

Understanding Your Business

After you've identified your ideal client you also need to identify some specific aspects of your business as well. You need to answer a few questions that will help you better market to your ideal audience. These are the questions I always ask clients and myself whenever marketing a product.

- What problem does your product or service solve?
- What pain or emotion is somebody feeling who needs this problem solved?
- What is the benefits of your product or service?
- What are the reasons people don't buy your product or service?
- What are the features of your product or service?
- How is your product different than your competition or service?
- What is your business mission statement?
- Who are your biggest competitors?
- Why would someone choose a competitor over you?

Knowing these Answers will help you in all aspects of marketing especially when it comes to writing ads, emails, making videos, and building sales pages.

Chapter 3

Don't go straight for the kiss

Applying that old saying

Have you ever heard someone talk about how you should treat customers like people, not customers. How do you do that? Great customer service certainly is important, but this is a marketing book, so let's focus on how to treat customers like people and not customers as marketers.

Treating the customer like a person is great advice. But how do you do it? You treat customers like people by dating them. I'm talking about the old fashioned way of dating, not one-night stands or blind dates. From start to finish you need to treat customers like you are dating them.

When you meet someone who you would like to date, what do you do? Do you walk right up to them and plant a big kiss right on the lips? Of course not! But why not? You might get smacked in the face, that's why.

This is the equivalent of showing ads directly to people and trying to get them to buy something when they have never even heard of you. Advertising to complete strangers is like kissing complete strangers. There is no trust or relationship built.

Will it work occasionally? Yes, but not often. If you try this route, you will spend lots of money and see little results.

Time to date

Marketing is like the dating process. It takes time and effort to convince people to trust you or your business. Some studies show that it takes seven touch points before someone is willing to buy from you. Whatever the number is, it takes time to build a relationship with complete strangers before they are willing to pull out their credit card and purchase something.

Think about when you are trying to date someone. Just like people have had bad dating relationships in the past, they have also have had bad experiences with businesses. That is the reason it can be hard to win them over.

What are the steps to building a relationship with potential customers? Just like dating, the concept is really simple. Once you understand these fundamentals you'll be ready to dive deeper.

To make this simple, let's break every step of dating down to the equivalent of the step in marketing. Now things like the pickup lines and where to put your hand on their back are all really important information. But most businesses aren't even getting people on the date. You have to walk before you can run, so let's start with getting people on the "date".

First, you need to know who you are interested in. Just like you need to know who your ideal client is. Do you like men or women? Blonde, brunette, or redhead? Tall or short? Skinny or thick? Blue eyes or brown? Fitness enthusiast or nerd?

This helps you identify who you want to spend your time talking to. There are other things to consider such as their personality and what they like to do for fun. These things you can identify before even talking to a person. If you like fit people, how do they dress? If you like people who are rock climbers, where do they hang out. This is why it is important to identify your ideal client before doing any marketing. That way you won't spend your time with the wrong type of people.

After you find the person you're interested in, you walk up to them and say hi. If they say hi back you engage in a conversation. If they don't and just ignore you, then you know they aren't interested and you go find someone else. This is like when you show your ads to people. With your advertisement, you're seeing who is interested in what you have to offer.

Once you get the conversation going you ask them for their phone number. If they say no, you know they aren't truly interested in you. At that point, you try a different approach or you go find someone else. This is like your landing page. You let them learn more about what you have to offer. You invite them to do something like opt-in for a free webinar or training. This is like when you ask for their number to go on a date.

It's great if you've asked someone out and they accepted. Unfortunately, just because they said yes and gave you their number doesn't mean they will show up. You have to text them or call them about the details. Maybe send reminders. You can also build the relationship by telling them more about yourself or asking them about themselves even before the first date.

Just like this dating routine, in marketing, after they opt-in you need to build this relationship with email or texting to get them to actually show up to whatever you are offering. Not every business has this exact module of having people show up to something, but they all have some form of it. You should rarely try to sell expensive products right away. I'll explain this more when I go over Lead Magnets.

Once you actually get someone on the date, you flirt, have a good time, and see if they are really interested in you. You test the waters, maybe try and hold their hand. You try to get them to see your value and that you're a pretty awesome person. The date is like when you do the training, webinar or whatever it is. You want to convince a potential customer that you are the best.

At the end of the date, you work up enough courage to go in for the kiss. You either get lucky and they kiss you back, or you have a very awkward moment you later lie about to your friends. This is when you finally try to sell or pitch your product. Yes, after all this work, time, and money you try and sell to them.

After they finally purchase something you are in a stage of continually dating or becoming "official". This stage is where you continue to build the relationship. You do this in order to try and bring them back to buy more. Just like with dating, you continue to build the relationship to the point of marriage, then kids etc.

This process can be over months or minutes. It depends on what type of product you sell and how much you charge. Higher priced products usually take longer than lower priced products.

Adjust as needed

You might be thinking that dating is not always so cut and dry, following an exact sequence. I understand dating is different for everyone. We all live different places with different cultures. The ideal date is different for everyone. Welcome to digital marketing! It's always different and changing, even if you've been doing the same business for years. Businesses and people change, or you offer a new product that needs to be marketed differently than your others.

That is why FIO is so important. You will continually need to learn and make adjustments to your marketing and strategy. There have been times I've sent people to a video or a blog where the opt-in waits for a certain amount of time to pass before it pops up. Sometimes I've done giveaways for clients that I wouldn't do for others. The main emphasis in marketing is building trust and relationships.

A new name for Marketers

"Of course I don't just randomly walk up to people and kiss them." This is what I hear most of the time when I use the comparison of this dating process to business owners. To be fair, it's common knowledge to avoid kissing strangers. But why do business owners and beginning marketers forget this is how humans work when we try marketing for the first time? Business to customer relationships are like human to human relationships and should be treated similarly.

Unsuccessful marketers skip the first steps of the dating process and go straight for the kiss. Does it work every so often? Yes, occasionally. But it's not dependable or sustainable. Think of the first steps of the dating process as warming up your audience.

If you get nothing else out of this book and just that principle I will consider it a success. The fundamental principle that is mostly forgotten is that digital marketing is all about building relationships. You need to figuratively date your customers. You need to warm them up before trying to sell to them. People don't trust businesses who obviously only care about making money.

Successful marketers should be called "Relationshippers". If you are focused on building relationships with people you will come across as genuine and real. Whether you are a service-based company or retail or online, building the relationship is the number one goal.

What about AdWords?

Maybe you've heard of Google AdWords. If you have, you're probably asking yourself how this marketing platform fits into building trust and relationships with people. If you don't know what Google AdWords is, simply put, it is a platform you use where you pay Google to show your website to someone when they search for specific phrases or words.

Don't worry, I will explain how this fits into building relationships and trust with people. For example, sometimes the dating process is sped up or you have less time to do it. To get a good idea, first look at when it's the right time to use Google AdWords.

Some people are ready to buy something right now and know exactly what they are looking for. When someone knows what they want or at least have a good idea of what they want, they are usually already looking for it somewhere. This is why Google AdWords is great for some businesses. Google AdWords is a marketing tool for customers who are searching for a specific product or solution.

This still fits into the idea of dating your potential customers and clients. Think about it. In dating, some people know what they want right now and they go look for it. They look to find people in places like dating apps, websites, or bars because they are ready to "buy".

No matter where you find your date, you still have to earn their trust, just like with any marketing. With tools like AdWords you just have less time to do it. There are a few tools that you'll have to use like social proof, establishing yourself as an authority and other methods. We'll get to those in the Landing Page chapter. No matter what you are selling you need to start with the relationship.

What about commercials?

So why do massive companies run commercials trying to sell things? Isn't that like walking up to a complete stranger and kissing them? Yes and no. The reason Nike or Apple can get away with this kind of marketing is they are like a celebrity. If you were famous and everyone knew who you were, you might be able to get away with kissing complete strangers.

When a business or brand is as big as Coke, they just need to reach as many people as they can. They have already built up relationships and trust with people. They just need you to see their ads to remind you about their product. They also have spent billions of dollars building up that trust already. If you have that kind of money, by all means, go run some commercials.

The 3E's

So what can you do as a business that doesn't have millions of dollars to spend on building trust and relationships? It's simple: create content.

There's a saying, "Content is king." I don't know who the person was that coined that phrase, but they are spot on. What it means is that content is the biggest thing that sells.

Think about it. What does the NBA sell? Yes, they sell tickets, jerseys, and autographs, but the real thing they sell is entertainment. These sports teams are bringing in billions and billions of dollars for something as simple as providing entertainment.

What does ESPN sell? The same entertainment but in a different format. They have a handful of different shows all dissecting a single game. They have articles and blogs, all of which are around a game someone else is playing.

People love their sports teams. To the point, they will get tattoos of their team logo and purchase jerseys and paraphernalia. Teams will disappoint their fans for years, but the fans still come back for more of that team's "content".

As a digital marketer you need to understand that your job is to provide content that will lead to sales. This content will be what helps you build trust and relationships with people, just like a sports team does with its fans.

Here is what you can do to get started in creating content. I call it the 3 E's:

Educate
Elevate
Entertain

With social media, videos, or whatever else you're doing, you should be using 1 - 3 of these E's before you try and sell a person anything. Doing these three things will help you connect and build a relationship with your potential customers.

Once you've built that relationship, you can then easily transition into selling your product or service. You are no longer a complete stranger and can move onto the "date".

There are a few things to remember when using the 3 E's:

1. All 3 E's should also be connected to your business's "Why". Your why is your mission statement or goal as a business. You could also call it your brand.
2. The 3E's should be used with your ideal client in mind.
3. The 3E's should be used in relation with what you sell.

Let's break down each of the 3E's and give some examples

Educate

Using educational posts or ads will help you establish yourself as an authority. When you establish yourself as the authority, it builds trust with people. They will listen to your advice and act on it. People will then come to you for advice, services, and products because you are the expert.

It's possible to build trust while educating people when you use something that complements your product. For example, if you sell dog grooming tools, you could teach how to properly groom a dog. Selling a weight loss supplement? Share five ways to lose fat. Try running a webinar on how to do X, Y, or Z.

This will help you transition into selling your product. When the education and the product you are selling connect, people will be drawn to what you are selling.

Another example is if I were trying to sell car parts and I first tried to educate readers on motorcycle repair. They are both motorized, and plenty of people who own a motorcycle own a car but they are unrelated. People who need motorcycle repair most likely don't need car repair as well.

Examples

- Quizzes
- Videos expanding on different topics
- Case studies
- Informational courses
- Product reviews
- Checklists
- Blueprints
- Blogs

Elevate

Content that elevates includes anything that inspires, motivates, or gets people to think deeper. This is great for connecting people to your mission statement as a business. It helps you form an emotional connection with people.

Gogogo...

You want to help people elevate their minds and their lives. Helping people feel inspired to do something good or motivated to work through the hard times is a great tool for marketing.

You want to find people who support your cause or mission. If you sell family or marriage counseling, then a video about families getting through tough times would be perfect. If you sell marshmallow sticks, show a video of people having a good time camping.

Ask yourself, "What is the emotion I want to bring to someone when they interact with my business?"

Examples:

- Anything that inspires, motivates, or gets people to think deeper
- Hype videos
- Inspirational quotes
- Success stories of overcoming adversity

Entertain

People want to be entertained. They will spend hours watching Netflix, Hulu, and YouTube. People love to laugh, cry, and even get scared, so use that to your advantage. Entertaining content is also more likely to be shared on social media sites by those who like them.

A key to using entertainment to build relationships with people is to make it relatable to what you sell. People think cat videos are funny, but that won't that help you sell life insurance. But if you sell skateboards, having a highlight reel of skateboarding tricks would be perfect.

You also have to keep in mind who your ideal client is. Some things that are entertaining to kids aren't entertaining to adults. Using gym memes when you sell fitness products work together great. You have to get in the mind of your ideal client to try and reach them.

Examples:

- Memes
- Funny videos
- Highlights
- Sketches
- Blogs

Pitfalls to Avoid

Any of the 3E's can be used incorrectly if not used for your ideal customers or in connection with your product. For example, I personally love gym memes. I follow three or four gym meme pages on Instagram.

What's interesting is that I can't imagine women liking one of these pages. It's not because women don't go to the gym, but the memes these accounts use are targeted to men. What blows my mind is this page sells mainly women's workout apparel. Now I can't see the data on their demographics, and

I haven't looked in their funnels, but selling women's apparel doesn't make sense. I look through the comments and the page likes and from what I see it's mostly from men.

They are using one of the 3E's (Entertain) with a product that doesn't match their ideal customer. I've said this multiple times, but whatever you're doing for the 3E's to build that trust, you need to have it in connection to your product and with your ideal customer in mind.

How to use them

All of the 3E's provide content that builds a relationship with your customers. You can use these in posts or in ads, on landing pages, and in emails. You can focus on one or all three of them. Just find the one that fits best with what your business represents and what you sell.

As you start using the 3E's and you've built trust and a relationship, you need to ask people to take action. Just like when you start engaging with someone to get them on a date, you need to actually ask them out. If you forget to ask them for their number or to actually set up the details, you'll never go on the date.

Remember when I talked about those free offers you see on social media? These businesses or people are asking you to watch a video, get a case study, learn more, or show up for a webinar. Many times they ask you to give them your name and email address. They are asking you on the "date".

They'll advertise that it's free, but remember that nothing on this earth is free. The price of that free product is your name and email. Just like when you get asked on a date, it isn't free. You may not be paying money, but it will cost time and your number.

In marketing, companies will try to build trust with you, and at the end of their webinar or video they do a sales pitch or "try to kiss you". It sounds like this, "Normally, you will get x, y, and z for X amount, but just for today it's Y amount". You see, they asked you on a date so they can get a good night kiss.

This isn't a bad thing, but it only works if they have built the relationship with you. If they offer value in the form of the 3E's they'll have a chance to gain you as a client. Imagine if they had skipped straight to the pitch in the ad; would you even click on it? Maybe if you are the 1 out of 1000. But the price would deter most people right off the bat.

If you give a company your name and email and you don't purchase their product, you will start getting a string of emails or something similar. These emails will be trying to convince you to give them another try or offer you more value. It's similar to going on one date and having your date ask you out again. I'll go into more detail about this follow-up strategy in the chapter on emails.

This is the universal strategy used by marketers to drive sales and leads. At its heart, if done correctly, it is built around establishing relationships with people. Once you have mastered this, it becomes much easier to start doing the steps of FIO.

Step 1: Try out an advertisement.

Step 2: Look at the data.

Step 3: Make adjustments.

Step 4: Repeat steps 1-3.

So this universal strategy is very simple

I've laid out the universal dating strategy, and hopefully you didn't get lost on the way. I fit a lot of details into a short amount of space. If you need to go back and reread this chapter, do it to make sure you clearly understand the information. I will be building off this chapter for the rest of the book.

It took me years to figure this all out on my own. I went to every webinar I could find and read what felt like every blog post written. I downloaded every eBook I could find, even if it didn't have very good ads or landing pages. I also had amazing mentors helping me and teaching me what makes great marketing.

There are gurus out there who are charging hundreds if not thousands of dollars to get this information. I don't want you to have to go through the same pain as I did trying to get the simple answers.

So here are the steps to an effective marketing strategy:

1. **Define your audience**: What is the kind of person you want to "date"?

2. **Show an ad**: Start talking to the person you're attracted to.

3. **Get them to a landing page**: Talk to people, tell them more about yourself, and try and to get them to agree to a date.

4. **Opt-in on a landing page for training, or a webinar, or video**: Ask for their phone number and ask them on a date.

5. **Get them to the training by following up**: Get them to show up for the date.

6. **Build value/deliver on training**: Have a great date.

7. **Sales pitch**: Go for the kiss.

8. **Continue to bring value/up-sell new products**: Continually date to become "official".

For those of you who are visual learners

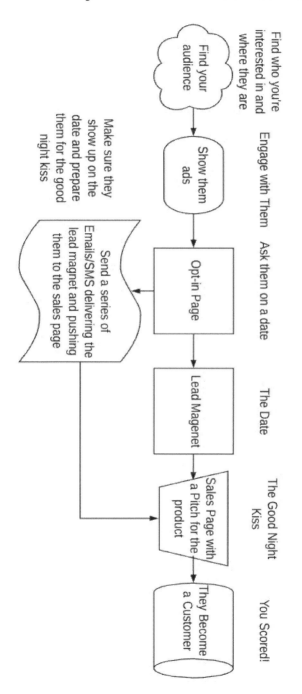

This is the perfect starting point for all marketing. Yes, you will have to make changes and FIO. This is not a foolproof plan because there is no such thing as a foolproof plan in marketing. However, this will help you springboard into making your marketing efforts effective.

Remember this strategy also can be adapted to and added on. Your product and business is different from everyone else's. You need to be able to adjust. This is your blueprint though. This is your starting point.

Unfortunately, this universal strategy will not always work. This is especially true if you do not have a quality product. People can see your weaknesses and issues with your product. You need to be able to bring value with whatever you are selling. If you don't have a quality product then stop reading this book and go fix your product first! In the next chapters I will be diving deeper into each step of this funnel. I will still be focusing on the fundamentals of each marketing tool and step. The chapters will follow the universal dating strategy.

Just know as I dive deep into social media that you need to look at it from several angles. For example, there are things in the social media chapter that will help on landing pages. Similarly, there is information about email marketing that also applies to social media. Information from SMS will go along with email marketing. Keep that in mind and continually ask yourself, "How can this help me in other areas?"

If you'd like a more indebt free training on the dating strategy you can get it here: www.thedigitalballer.com/amazon I'll walk you through this strategy step by step.

Chapter 4

Growing a Social Media Following

I'm excited to examine social media with you. I majored in social media marketing. It's where I found my love for digital marketing. One of the biggest things I learned was that you need to go where the people are.

For instance, imagine if you were a chiropractor. Pretend you have an invitation to two different parties. The first is a big party for anyone who has hurt their back. The second party is for people who have amazing, healthy backs. Which party would you attend? You'd probably go to the first party. Not only that, but you'd probably set up a booth, hand out fliers, and offer free adjustments to get people to come back to you for more.

You wouldn't go to the second party where everyone has amazing, healthy backs at all. Why? Because that second party is **NOT** where **YOUR IDEAL** people are. The first party **HAS YOUR IDEAL** people. This also applies to the different social media platforms.

Almost everyone is on some sort of social media platform. It is getting easier and easier to find people on them. Find out what social media platform *your* ideal client is on and go get them.

The Winds Of Change

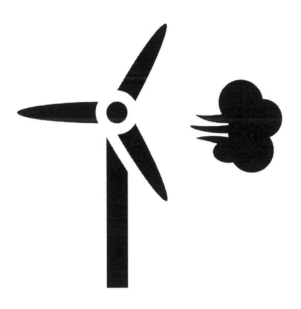

As you learn how to use social media for your digital marketing strategy, you'll come to find out it's an ever-changing tool. Every month you'll need to learn something new and make adjustments. Things that worked at the beginning of social media marketing no longer do. You'll have to be able to adapt and change.

The dating strategy, however, continues to hold strong. The reason it keeps working is because humans like to be treated like humans. Whatever strategy you use on any social media platform, you will still need to use the principles of the dating strategy. One of the most important things is to remember to stay disciplined. Don't skip steps, or go for the goodnight kiss when you first meet them.

I've often heard business owners say, "I tried doing Facebook but I didn't see anything come from it." I don't blame them for being skeptical of social media marketing. It's not like a billboard where you can see a physical product. They might have spent $1,000 dollars on Facebook ads and didn't make a single dollar back.

Here is why most business owners don't see results right away. Social media is a long-term game. You are running a marathon, not running sprints. Can you and will you get lucky and see results quickly? Yes, sometimes, if done right.

Making a social media account and just posting things doesn't work *if* you do it without purpose. There are a lot of people going nowhere fast.

Your goal should be using the 3E's to start building relationships with people. Most of the time, social media is the first two stages of the dating process: identifying who your ideal client is and introducing yourself.

First thing first

What is the first thing you should do when getting started with social media marketing? It is *not* posting videos or pictures. It is *not* inviting all of your friends to like the page or to follow you. The first thing you need to do is set up whatever kind of tracking code or pixel provided on your website.

For Facebook and Instagram, it's called the Facebook Pixel. Google has one. Snapchat and Pinterest have one. Whatever platform you use, it is essential to get that piece of code and put it on your website.

You need to do this because that code helps you start identifying your ideal clients. It will track who comes to your website. It can give you data on the demographics of who visits. It can tell you genders, ages, locations, ethnicities, and more. It can even tell you what other pages your site visitors like so you can do more research. The more you know about your customers, the better you will write ads targeted to them.

Have you ever seen tons of ads for a company after visiting their website? That is because that piece of code allows them to have their ads follow people who come to their website. The ability to show ads to people who have already been to your website is helpful to push them over the edge of deciding if they should buy or not. They are people who already know who you are and are farther along in the dating process.

This code will also help you track how well your ads are doing. You will be able to see how many sales or leads came directly from that platform. You'll know what ads are performing well and what ads stink. This is essential for FIO when you are testing and tweaking ads.

Let me break down social media marketing for you. There are two main ways to use social media: paid ads and organic content. Both have value, drawbacks, and overlap each other. To get the most out of social media you'll need to use both. I'll break down both sides and how to properly use them.

Organic Social Media

Organic social media is the posts or videos you make to your page or profile. Unlike ads, your posts can be seen without putting money behind them. They should be less about selling something and more about building a relationship.

With organic social media, most people don't understand the purpose or have a goal in mind when using it. When you don't know the goal, you'll make posts without any endgame in mind. Posting randomly and without an objective will get you nowhere fast. Direction is more important than speed. Not knowing your goal in using organic social media will stop you from seeing the value it can bring. If you're not seeing the value you might think about quitting before making any progress.

Your objective with organic social media is to build a following or community. This will lead to increasing your brand awareness. You want to get in front of as many people as possible. Just like when you are trying to find a date, you need to talk to as many people as you can.

Using organic social media will help you to start building a relationship with people. You don't want your business to be a stranger to people. You want them to know and trust you.

Organic social media can be two stages in the dating strategy. The first stage is like introducing yourself to new potential dates. You're warming up your audience. You are seeing who connects with your brand. You are introducing yourself to like-minded individuals.

The second stage you could be using it for is continually dating current customers. This is where you can strengthen a relationship with people to get them to continue to come back for more. Your work isn't done after the first sale. Continuing and building this relationship will increase the lifetime value of your customers.

Everything I'll explain in this chapter will be more focused on the first stage of finding new customers. That is where most business owners time and attention is needed. Just know that this information is also applicable to the stage of continually dating your current customers.

What do I even post?

Now I get asked all the time, "What should I post?" The answer is simple: the 3E's. People want social media to be social. They want to be entertained.

They don't think to themselves, "I need some new shoes, so I better go look on Snapchat." But if they have connected with your brand on social media, and you have continually built value with them using the 3E's, then when they are ready to buy shoes they will think of you. Again, social media is a long game.

Someone could have started following you a year before actually buying anything. People are all in different places when it comes to your product and aren't always ready to buy. If you are consistently building trust and relationships, eventually you'll create a steady stream of leads and customers.

With organic posts, you should rarely sell your products. Remember, with organic, you are building your community of followers and fans with the 3E's. Yes, your product can still be in those posts, but you should rarely post with the intent of selling your product. You need to build trust! People don't like the idea of someone constantly trying to sell to them.

I like to keep a five to one posting ratio. For every five pieces of content using the 3E's, you can share a promotional post. Until you have some sort of following, keep it to just 3E's posts.

Breaking down Social Media Posts/Ads

With most social media platforms, when you make an organic post, there are two components. I say *most social media* because there are so many different social media sites and platforms, and they constantly change. The first component is the picture/video. The second component is the message. Both are important in different ways.

The picture or video will snag people's attention to get them to stop. Your goal is to get them to stop scrolling and to take a few seconds of their day to look at what you have to say. The message will help you connect with them. Both need to work together in order to help you reach your goal.

Let's break down both parts of an organic post by focusing on simple fundamentals that will get you started in the right direction. Once you really get the hang of it, you can then look to find more in-depth tips and tricks that work great for your industry or the type of business you run. It all comes back to the four steps of FIO.

Social Media Copywriting

Let's look at the message first. I prefer writing the message and then finding the best picture to fit the message. Usually, I find it easier to find stock pictures that reflect the message than to write a message based on the picture. Or I have the message in mind when I get the picture taken because I know what I want it to look like.

You might find that doing the opposite works better for you. That's fine; you just need to find what works best for your business and your style. Try both and find out what way you like through FIO.

The words or message you put behind the picture or video is known in the marketing world as copywriting. Your purpose with the message is to connect with potential followers and build that relationship. So speak to them like you would in person. Write like you talk. This isn't your high school history report. Don't misspell words, but don't worry as much about the grammar. You want to make this as easy to read as possible.

Your message should get people to feel some emotion or do something simple. You want people to engage with you so that your post gets seen by more people. Social media platforms want their users to see the best content possible. Social media is programmed to promote posts with a lot of engagement. If you get more engagement, you will get more people seeing your posts.

Every person has their group of people or a bubble of influence. As someone likes or shares a post, it will also be shown to some of the people in their bubble of influence. So the more engagement generated, the more bubbles of influence your post will appear in.

A great way to get people to engage is to ask them a question. A big mistake I see businesses make is when they ask a question and they just leave it at that. You should also tell them to leave the answer in the comments or leave a like if they agree. What's the point of asking a question if you don't want an answer?

Don't be afraid to ask people to act by commenting, liking, or sharing. When you ask people to do something, remember to tell them *why* they should. "Leave a like if chest day is your favorite day!" "Comment below what your favorite hairstyle is." Or "Share this to get the word out about the zombie apocalypse." Whatever you're asking them to do, tell them why they should do it.

Your copy should be connected to the picture or video. If you are writing about a dog and you use a picture of a cat, it doesn't make sense. I know that seems like a no-brainer, but I've seen so many times where the copy and the image have nothing to do with each other.

A few fundamentals with social media copywriting to remember:

- Write like you talk.
- Get people to engage by liking, sharing, or commenting.
- Tell people why they should engage.
- Connect the copy to the picture or video.

Pictures

When choosing your pictures for social media, here are a few quick suggestions to help. The picture you use needs to be nice quality. Be sure the pictures aren't blurry, that they don't have part of people's heads cropped out, and that they are real.

Real pictures aren't just shots of your product. For example, no one wants to see photos of just a book. People would rather see pictures of people reading books. Pictures of backpacks are lame, but pictures of people on a mountain top with a backpack are awesome.

If you don't have a high-quality camera that's ok. High quality photos on social media are more about not being blurry. Most smartphone cameras will do the trick. People like real, not necessarily professional photos.

Think of the last picture you liked on social media. Why did you like it? What was it about? Was it your friend, or a celebrity? Continually analyze pictures you see on social media that have a lot of engagement (likes, comments, and shares) to improve your own photos, aka FIO.

A few fundamentals with pictures:

- Don't post blurry pictures.
- Don't partially crop heads.
- Posts pictures of people doing things or using the products or objects, not just pictures of objects.
- Use photos that stand out. Your goal is to get people to stop and look.

Video

If I ever have a choice between using a video or a picture, I use a video. They are more engaging and can snag people's attention better than images. Many of the social media sites or platforms also prefer video over pictures. What I mean by that is their algorithm will cause videos to show to more people than pictures will.

Video also gives you a few more elements than pictures do.

The first element that you get with video is music. You can use music to create emotion and get people to feel things. Watch a scary movie without music and you'll see how important music is. The movie will almost become comical.

The second element needed for video is putting emotion and feeling into your words. With video, you can articulate your message with a feeling or tone of voice that can reach a tougher audience. You can also emphasize different points more heavily than others.

The third element present in video is authenticity. People can see the real you or put a face to your business. This can build trust faster because people get to see the face behind the words.

The first three seconds of a video are crucial. You have very little time to grab a viewer's attention. Don't waste time on some kind of intro. Use a question or fact right away to grab their attention and get them to stay.

You want to get people to stop what they are doing and watch. Another good way to grab attention is to put subtitles in the video. This will help snag people's attention and get them to stick around longer.

Sometimes people forget to use subtitles in their videos. You should always include them because not everyone has their sound on while they are on social media. If they are at work and aren't supposed to be on social media, they probably won't have their sound on. Don't give them a reason not to watch your video.

A few fundamentals of using videos on social media.

1. Keep them short: people don't have long attention spans.
2. Use subtitles always: people won't always turn the sound on.
3. Do something special or interesting in the first three seconds of the video.
4. Leave intros out altogether, or at least wait until after you've snagged their attention.

Stick to the schedule

Trying to remember what and when to post can be a chore. If you try and post every few days without a plan, you'll most likely forget to do it after a while. One of the keys of organic social media is consistency. Something that will help you stay consistent is to make a social calendar. Simply decide what days you will post and the type of post you will publish.

Example:

Monday: An educational post
Tuesday: Funny meme
Wednesday: Nothing
Thursday: Inspirational quote
Friday: Nothing
Saturday: Video Q&A

Luckily you don't have to wait for the day of to make your post. Some social media platforms will let you schedule posts out. If the platform you are using doesn't, then there is plenty of software that does. This way, everything will go out on time and this lets you focus on other aspects of your business.

All that work for nothing?

A common misconception for new people getting into social media is that your post will be shown to anyone who likes your page or follows you. Unfortunately, that isn't true. Social media sites and platforms want the best and most relevant content shown to their users.

This is why you want to get as much engagement as you can. The more engagement a post gets, the more the social media platform knows you made a great post, and they will show it to more people. When you make a post and it gets a lot of engagement, that's a sign it was a great post.

When you have a great post, you can boost it (put money behind it) to get it shown to even more people. In the chapter on data, I'll give you some standards to measure if your post is getting a lot of engagement.

Final Thoughts

The most important thing you can remember about organic social media is to make posts using the 3E's. You are trying to build relationships with people. You don't even have to use your own content. Sharing content from other sources such as blog posts and videos will help you get started. Creating content can take time; you don't have to post every day, but you do have to post consistently.

With organic posts, your goal is to build a community. Something to remember is that communities talk to each other. Don't be afraid to engage with your audience and followers.

When someone comments on your post, like it or reply to them. Just like when you're dating someone and they text you, you need to text them back. Not with just a "Haha". That isn't how you build a relationship. Treat them like you would your friends and family.

Don't be afraid if someone writes a negative comment. We like to call those "trolls", and they are everywhere. No matter what you do, the trolls will find a way to make nasty comments. You can use it as an opportunity to show your customer service.

Social media is a great way to help with your customer service. It goes back to the concept that people want to be treated like people. If you handle situations well, other people notice and it makes you look better.

Remember that growing your social media at the beginning is tough, especially if you don't have a massive budget. A simple way to grow your audience at little cost is through collaborations.

Getting on bigger pages who already have a huge following is great for getting you in front of new people. They have already spent the time to build a relationship with their community. When they collaborate with you it will help their community more likely trust you.

With organic social media, your goals are to:

- Build a community of followers
- Start to make a relationship with potential customers
- Be consistent with posting content
- Continue to build your existing relationship with current customers
- Collaborate with others

Chapter 5

Paid Social Media Ads

Paid ads are slightly different from organic posts. The social media platform usually will distinguish the two differently by putting the word "sponsored" or "ad" somewhere in your post. Where organic posts are free, ads are only shown when you pay the social media platform.

Why pay for ads?

So why use ads over posts? It would seem like organic content is better than ads. Isn't free better than having to pay? Yes and no. It comes back to what you are trying to accomplish and what the best way is to get there.

Consider that although organic posts are free, not everyone will see them. For example, with Facebook, you may have 1000 people who have liked your page. But when you make a post, only 150 people will see it. If you really want everyone to see your post, you would have to pay Facebook to get it shown to everyone. So it really isn't 100% free.

With organic posts, you can't test things and make adjustments like with ads. With ads, you can test different audiences, see what copy works best, and determine which picture gets more people's attention. You want to be able to FIO, and it's more difficult and time consuming to test with organic posts.

Organic posts stay up longer for people to see. This sounds great, but it may end up being a disadvantage. There are times you don't want everyone to see some promo or special you are no longer running. Ads give you a chance to change things up.

While running ads you want to be able to track results. With Facebook, for example, you are able to see how many people who saw or clicked on an ad performed a specific action on your website. On the other hand, with an organic post you don't get any info such as opting in for a free trial, purchasing a product, or downloading content. You need to be able to see and track what is working and what isn't.

With ads, you can target people who have come to your website. In order to retarget people who come to your website, you'll need the code that the social media platform provides you. This is all possible with running ads. If you want faster success than the long game of organic social media, paid ads will help get you there quicker.

Get the Fire Going

Remember when I said you do not want to go up to strangers and kiss them? Organic posts are a great way to introduce yourself and warm people up. They'll then know who you are, and you are beginning to build the relationship. This is why you can use both ads and organic content together to have success in social media marketing.

If you don't have a following already, you can use ads to attract potential followers. Using a video in an ad is also a great way to attract followers and start warming up an audience. You can retarget anyone who has watched a certain amount of your organic videos or video ads. Someone who stuck around and watched 50-100% of your video is a warmer lead and a better place to invest both time and money.

You can also run ads to your blog post and retarget those people who read it. You can also advertise lead magnets. However you choose to warm up people, remember why you are doing it. You are building your relationship with them.

Lead Magnets

With your ads, your goal is to get people to act a specific way. You want them to go to your landing page or website to do something. You usually accomplish this with some kind of lead magnet.

A lead magnet is something you use to pull people in, just like a magnet will pull metal closer to it. The lead magnet is the "date" you would take someone on.

Some great lead magnets are:

- eBooks
- Webinars
- Free Training
- Free Courses
- Blogs

- Video Series
- Quizzes
- Free Quotes

I won't go into the details of each of these lead magnets, but there are a few things that help make them successful. They need to be free or less than $49 . How much you charge depends on your ideal client, your main product, and how big your budget is.

If you sell a low-priced product or service, have ideal clients with a low budget, and have a smaller marketing budget, then you should generally stick to free lead magnets.

If your ideal clients are big spenders, your main product is high-priced, and you have a much bigger budget, you can get away with charging up to $49. Most businesses should keep their lead magnets free. You are trying to get a lead, not a sale.

All you need from the lead source is to get their name, email, and or phone number. This information is extremely valuable. Once you get their name, number, or email you can continually market to them almost for free. Email marketing and SMS marketing aren't completely free but they are much cheaper than ads.

You build your list so you can continue to build a relationship with potential customers more intimately. Just like when you ask someone on a date, you also need their name and number. This way you can connect and build a relationship before and after the date.

I'll get into more detail about email and SMS marketing in the later chapters, but your goal with your ads and lead magnets is to get people's information in an honest and forthright way. It's similar to how you would get someone on a date.

Body Parts of an Ad

With ads, there are four parts: the headline, the copy, the image/video, and the call to action. The rules for the copy and image in ads are the same as for the organic posts.

The headline should be a sneak peak of the copy, summarized into a simple question or statement. Your headline should be something that leads into the copy. Headlines are supposed to grab people's attention and get them interested. If you want to see amazing headlines, go to the grocery store and look at the magazines.

Magazines are great at getting people's attention. They have been doing it for years and have figured out what works. Take some of the headlines you see there and put in your own product or wording.

Don't copy them word for word of course, but look at keywords they used and the words they left out. Your goal is to learn what works best for you and your business. But take any chance you can to learn how to make eye-grabbing headlines.

Copywriting for ads is similar to writing copy for organic posts. I will get into writing copy for ads in the email chapter. Many of the principles apply to both emails and ads.

Your ad copy needs to lead people to the call to action or CTA. The CTA should take them to your landing page or website to get more information or to claim the lead magnet. Tell them why they should use the CTA just like with organic posts. Make it clean and easy to see what they need to do.

Writing Your First Ad

When it comes to writing your first ad, you need to keep two things in mind. First, who is your ideal audience? Second, keep in mind the list of questions you asked yourself back in chapter two about understanding your business. They are:

- What problem does your product or service solve?
- What pain or emotion is somebody feeling who needs this problem solved?
- What are the benefits of your product or service?
- What are the reasons people don't buy your product or service?

- What are the features of your product or service?
- How is your product or service different from that of your competition?
- What is your business's mission statement?
- Who are your biggest competitors?
- Why would someone choose a competitor over you?

Knowing the answers to these questions will make writing ads much easier. Keep in mind that the format for writing ads is different on every platform. For example, some platforms only allow a certain number of words, whereas other platforms will let you write as much as you want. Some platforms might not let you use words in the image, whereas other platforms will.

Even though the format of the ads is different, the fundamentals of writing ads remains the same across all platforms.

Here is a basic checklist of everything an ad needs so that you can get started:

- Address the pain point
- Offer a clear solution
- Help people self-identify as your ideal audience
- Social proof (you'll learn about in the next chapter)
- Show you're an authority (you'll learn about in the next chapter)

- The call to action

Testing Your Ad

There are many facets of an ad that you can test. You can try long copy or short copy. Try putting emojis or no emojis. Try bolding some words and not bolding others. Your purpose is to see what works the best with the audience you show your ads to.

Try multiple types of pictures. You can see if the image of a woman does better than the image of a man. Does a picture of a family or a picture of a couple work better? Your goal is to FIO with your ads by continually testing and seeing what works.

Just remember you need to test everything. Then you need to go through the steps of FIO.

Step 1: Try an advertisement out.

Step 2: Look at the data.

Step 3: Make Adjustments.

Step 4: Repeat steps 1-3.

If something isn't working and you don't like the results, you make adjustments. I like to first try changing the picture. Then I make changes to the headline. If that isn't working, then I visit the copy, after that I look deeper at the audience I'm targeting.

Final thoughts on ads

Running social media ads is extremely important to digital marketing. They do take time to learn and master. It will be expensive and you won't be perfect. But if you're willing to invest in paid social ads, it can do wonders for your business.

There are so many social media platforms out there it will be hard to decide which one to use. You'll hear from gurus and experts that certain platforms are better than others. What I say to that is "Whatever!" with a big eye roll.

There are so many platforms out there, and there are even more industries. There isn't a one-size-fits-all social platform that gets everyone. You need to find which one will work best for you and your business. The best way to decide which is the best platform is to find out which platform has your ideal audience. Once you find the one, try and learn everything you can about it.

Final Thoughts on Social Media

During the time I was working for the software company, I was talking to a good friend of mine who had built a rather impressive multi-million dollar ecommerce store. The main platform he was using was Google AdWords. He was killing it. He also thought Google AdWords was the place to be, and everyone should be using it. We both thought he could help the company I was working for with marketing our software on Google AdWords, so we made arrangements to get it all started.

The next week I was at an event running a booth, and I met a guy interested in our software. After hearing about it, he asked me what we were doing for advertising. I explained we were running Facebook ads, and we were also about to turn on some Google AdWords. He instantly threw up his hands and said, "Don't waste your time on Google AdWords! It doesn't work!"

A little confused, I asked him why. He went on to say that it was super over-priced, and no one was seeing results like they used to. He went on to tell me all about "big data". Long story short, being the young marketer I was, I chased what he was selling.

Through his "big data" he started sending us leads for us to sell our software. Five thousand dollars later, we didn't even have a single sale for our best sales rep who had a 60% close rate. Not to mention that 75% of the leads were wrong numbers.

At the same time, we ran ads on Google AdWords through my friend. He started generating quality leads at $10 per lead. So Google AdWords actually worked well for us.

The lesson was learned. Find the platform that works best for you. Maybe it's Facebook ads and maybe it's not. Find what works for you and FIO.

If you'd like a 100% FREE training on how to Identify where your audience is you can get it here: www.thedigitalballer.com/amazon I'll walk you through how to identify what advertising platform is right for you.

Chapter 6

Landing Pages and Websites

Now that we have talked about social media, we need to talk about the next step, where you send viewers after they click on your ad. In the digital marketing world, this is what is referred to as traffic.

A common misconception is that ads sell your products. False. They help with getting the sell by sending traffic to your product's page. What sells your products is your landing page or website. The only objective of the ad is to send traffic to your landing page or website.

Your ad is like a flyer telling people about your party. Once people get to your party the flyer has done its job. The quality of the party is what sells people on staying at the party. Similarly, your landing page or website sells your traffic on your product.

Landing page or website?

What should you use? A landing page or a website. First, I believe very few businesses need a fully developed, extremely nice website. The reason is most people won't find your website unless they know the exact URL. There are countless websites, and it takes a lot of work to be found by strangers without ads. People will waste thousands of dollars making a website look great but have little to no traffic coming to it.

Just as organic social media and running social media ads are different, so are landing pages and websites. Both have benefits and should be used in different situations.

Websites are like your digital store. It's where people can look around and take their time. Websites have a menu to navigate everywhere. You can write your blog posts there. It is a great place to tell people about your business.

You can have all of your business information there in one place. It also makes you look more professional and helps establish yourself as an authority and real business. Also, when someone has heard of you and does a search specifically for you, they'll have a chance to find you.

Websites work well with organic social media. Your community or following know who you are, and they can come to your website to get more information. Just like if you had a store in the mall, people come in to look around, find what they want and buy it, or they leave.

Landing pages are different in the fact that they should only have one purpose or action for the visitor. Everyone you send to this landing page should only go there so they can do or get one thing. You don't want any menus or blog posts here to distract viewers from your purpose.

Landing pages are like setting up a booth at an event. You have a lead magnet, special offer, or one product you are promoting. You don't have all your products out. You want people to do one thing only.

For example, when I was the Director of Marketing for the software company, we sponsored many events. We would go and set up booths to get leads for our product. We did really well at these events because we focused on the principles of the "dating" strategy, building relationships, networking, and getting leads rather than making sales.

This worked great because we only went to events where our ideal clients were. Go where the right kind of people are. We made some mistakes and went to some events that didn't have our ideal clients, and we made very few sales from those events.

In our booth, we had a big jar of cash. We had a sign, aka our ad, giving the instructions. It was simple: opt-in through our texting platform for a chance to win the cash.

That cash was our lead magnet, aka asking someone on a date. If the sign got their attention, they would stop. If it didn't, they would just keep on walking.

It was a great attention-getter, and we had plenty of people stopping and opting in. This allowed us a chance to talk to them, find out more about them, and start building relationships. The important thing was that we also got their information when they opted in.

At the end of the event, we would announce the winners. By this time, we also would have set up some free SMS marketing consultations with several people, aka gotten them on a date. For anyone who opted in but didn't schedule a consultation, we would send emails/texts following up with them to try to schedule one.

At the end of their SMS marketing consultations, we would pitch our product, aka going for the kiss. We made a lot of money from these events because we followed the same strategy we followed when running ads. The Dating Strategy doesn't just apply to digital marketing.

The booth was like our landing page simple and with one focus. We offered people something free in exchange for their information, which got them on a path with only our one goal in mind. For this book, I will be focusing on the fundamentals of landing pages and not websites.

Fundamentals of websites could fill a whole book. Because websites can be very complex, you usually need someone else to build your website for you. Most landing page software are simple enough that anyone can use them, even without coding experience.

Most of the fundamentals for landing pages can be applied to your website as well, if that's the direction you choose to go. They also apply to other areas of digital marketing such as ads or emails.

Choose one or try both

There are two types of landing pages: long and short. In a long landing page, you put as much information on it as you can. You put only the most important information into short landing pages. Which one works better? Who knows? It's different for every single business and product. That is why FIO is so important.

If your product is complicated or more expensive, try a long landing page at first. This way potential clients can gain a better understanding and get more information. You can give more details to help persuade people to buy.

If you're using a free lead magnet to start building a relationship with potential clients, start with a short landing page and evaluate the number of email opt-ins. If you don't see a high number of opt-ins (that will be covered in chapter 9), then start to expand on your landing page.

You need to test everything. Try both long and short pages and evaluate which works the best. One of the biggest mistakes marketers can make is to assume they know it all and don't look at the data. Data doesn't lie, and you won't get the data till you test. Just like when you FIO with ads, you need to FIO with your landing pages.

Formatting your LP

Whether you do long or short landing pages, you still need to follow some fundamentals. The first fundamental to understand is that your prime real estate is at the top of the page. People don't always scroll down. All of the most important information needs to be at the top.

The top of your page should state exactly <u>what problem you solve</u> and <u>how you solve it.</u> People buy because they feel an emotion, and it's usually a painful one. They have a problem and need to fix it with something. Your product needs to be that solution.

You need to tell people what problem you solve and exactly how you are going to solve I, as quickly and in the simplest way possible. This is not where you list the features of your product or service.

There is a time and a place for explaining the features of your product, which I will discuss later in this chapter.

Here are a few ways to structure the top of your landing pages:

- Address the pain you solve with a question. Directly underneath the question, tell how to fix that pain.
- Sum up exactly what problem you solve with one to three clear benefit statements underneath.

Example 1

If I was selling a high quality skateboard to people who have tons of experience, it would look something like this:

Sick of your skateboards not lasting?
You'll never have that problem again.
We have the highest quality skateboard on the market!

We targeted the pain someone would have. And we told them simply how we would solve it. This wording would change depending on who your ideal customer is. When I am coming up with headlines like this, I first write out all the problems my product solves. Then I consider the questions I would ask someone to figure out if they have those problems, and then I list as many ways as possible to tell someone how I can fix their problem.

Example 2

If I was trying to sell a skateboard to someone who was looking to get into skateboarding, it would look something like this:

Looking for an exciting hobby?

- Feel freedom from your cares as you coast down the road
- Get where you need to go faster than if you ran
- Look stylish as a boss

These are benefits people will get by buying a skateboard. It's clear, simple, and easy to read. Don't write big paragraphs, as people might get overwhelmed and skip right over them.

You aren't writing a book or an essay for potential customers. You need to throw out your old English teacher's advice. You need to make everything simple and easy to read. Your goal is to communicate exactly what people will get as clearly and succinctly as possible.

Benefits are not Features

One of the biggest mistakes I see in marketing is when people try to sell a feature and not a benefit. They can be very similar, so they are easy to mix up.

Most of the time people don't buy products because of features. The odds are other companies have the same or similar features that you have. However, the features are solving a problem, and you have to show how that problem is solved through your benefit statements.

Consider the example of the skateboard. What are the features of a skateboard? It has:

- Wheels
- Grip Tape
- Wood

These are pretty obvious features.

So the wrong way to market it would be something like:

- Our boards have amazing wheels
- We have the best grip tape
- We use quality wood for the board

The same can be said about every skateboard. But this is how some marketers would try and sell it. That will not be appealing for most people. They can get those features anywhere and possibly find a cheaper deal.

What if the landing page said something like:

- Never be late again! Get around faster than all your friends who walk
- Feel what it's like flying without being on an airplane
- Girls love bad boys what better way to show you are one than on a skateboard!

This is the same product, but one sounds much more fun and useful. These are clear benefits of getting a skateboard. They are clearly showing solutions from which skateboard owners benefit.

Features do have their place. People still want to know them. But they shouldn't be the main focal point of your landing page.

After someone has read your benefit statements, your landing page should lead people to a Call to Action.

The CTA

Your call-to-action should be the center of attention after your benefit statements. You need people to easily see what to do and how to do it. You should have a call-to-action at the top of your landing page, next to or right below your benefit statements.

A longer landing page should also have your call-to-action repeated two or three times throughout. People make the mistake of leaving the call-to-action at the bottom of the page where most people never see it. If you have your CTA multiple times through the landing page, the odds of someone taking action go up significantly.

Red means STOP

Another quick fundamental is your call-to-action button. Make it green, orange, gold, or bright blue. Color makes a difference. Those are usually the best performing colors, but test them out. Just stay away from red. Red is like stop signs and red lights, and red communicates to people to stop.

There is enough science and research behind colors to fill books, but if you want to research it more, go ahead. What is more important is you need to FIO for your product. Test different colors out. That is how you get in the mindset of a marketer. Just FIO.

Little things can make the difference. You should always be looking for ways to improve your marketing efforts. Button color is just one little aspect.

Stop in the name of the law!

Another fundamental of landing pages is to show you are an authority. Tell people why you are the best. It is ok to brag about yourself. They need to know you know what you are doing. You have to be like the male peacock and show your feathers! This is also applicable to websites and in social media.

Do you want someone helping you buy a house who has never helped someone before? Or do you want a seasoned veteran? Just like when I, at the beginning of the book, told you some of my accomplishments. If I want you to trust me as a digital marketer, you need to know some of my successes.

I could have also shared that one of my SMS marketing strategies has generated over 10 million dollars and counting in increased revenue for one of the companies where I consulted. This example may sound like bragging, but it shows that I've had experience and success in digital marketing.

The more experience you can mention, the better. I heard one marketer share they have spent over $500,000 on Facebook ads. They did this so they could show that they have experience and know what they are talking about. That is a big number and sounds impressive.

Some other examples are: "I have 2000 hours of personal training experience.", or "I've been doing this the last 20 years." Use whatever you can do to show you have experience.

Just don't be dishonest. Nothing can break a relationship faster than lying. If you have zero experience, find a different way to show you know what you are doing.

Showing you are an authority is a fundamental aspect of all marketing, not just in landing pages but also in your ads, emails, and even billboards.

Prove it

The next fundamental element of your landing page is social proof. Social proof and showing you are an authority are very similar and go hand-in-hand. Showing you are an authority comes from you. Social proof, on the other hand, boosts what you claim by coming from others. It's one thing to say you're the best at something, but it's another when others back you up.

A way to look at social proof is like what you might do when choosing a restaurant. What would you choose between, a busy looking restaurant or one that was as empty as a graveyard at midnight? Sometimes you'll try the empty one, but most likely you will choose the busy one. It's busy for a reason. Subconsciously that connects with being better.

Social proof takes the form of reviews and testimonials. I've heard some horror stories from people who have been scammed and tricked when buying things online. Having reviews from other people that have already purchased a product can give a feeling of safety. It helps customers make the decision to buy. People generally don't want to be the first to try something.

You need to show people that others have found success, joy, results, or whatever your product or service brings to them.

A great example is something like:

This book has helped thousands of entrepreneurs learn the skills of becoming a digital baller! Just take the word of John!

"This book helped me finally understand marketing! I've spent so much time and money trying to find out where to start, but now I have the foundation to move forward!"

You should have at least three testimonials on your landing pages. It's so important to always be asking customers for reviews so you have this ammo. The more to choose from the better.

Use reviews on your landing page that go with your benefit statements. One way you can get reviews like that is when you ask for a review, give them an example. Coaching your clients or customers through reviews will help you get the best reviews possible.

Speak now or forever hold your peace

Another great fundamental is to add scarcity to your offer. You can use phrases such as: "For a limited time only!" or "While supplies last!". Or add a countdown timer so people can see that time is running out. This will help them realize they need to act now.

Scarcity can help people make the commitment. If they are sitting on the fence about purchasing your product, letting them know the price will go up or the free trial will go away will help them be more decisive. If there is no sign of the deal or offer going away anytime soon, they might take their time to act.

Pricing to perfection

One last simple fundamental is pricing. $9.99 looks better than $10. $49.99 looks better than $50. If you're not convinced, look at every restaurant menu.

So here is a breakdown of all the fundamentals for landing pages:

- Keep the most important info at the top
- Provide benefit statements rather than a list of features
- Show you are an authority
- Have social proof
- Add scarcity
- FIO, test EVERYTHING

There is so much to consider for landing pages. A huge part of landing pages is the sales page. A sales page is the landing page you sell your product on. If you'd like my Sale Page Blueprint go to www.thedigitalballer.com/amazon to get it for FREE. This will help you get more examples and help with building high-converting landing/sales pages.

Chapter 7

Email isn't dead yet

"Email is dead! Nobody checks it anymore. It is a waste of time. Don't even bother." This is what I hear all of the time. But is it true?

Email, like all marketing tools, can be effective if used correctly. I don't believe email marketing is dead. I believe people suck at email marketing. I've seen amazing results from email marketing, even today.

Is email marketing as effective as it was 20 years ago? No, but 20 years ago there weren't spam and promotion folders blocking your email. The longer you do marketing you'll learn that everything is in a continual state of change. Part of the reason is that marketers ruin everything.

Marketers have a bad reputation for ruining every new tool they can get their hands on. I should clarify. Marketers ruin everything when they don't use marketing tools like they should and skip steps of building relationships.

With email, for example, marketers started buying lists of emails and blasting people's email. They overused it and forced companies like Google to block unwanted emails. People's inboxes got so overcrowded they stopped opening emails altogether.

Because of this, email open rates are very low compared to what they used to be. It now takes more skills than ever before to get your emails noticed and opened.

That doesn't mean that it's impossible. You can still have success using email marketing. If you use email in the right place and at the right time it can still be a high-converting tool.

Why use it?

If email open rates are so low, why should you use it?

One reason you should still use email is that you can get more information in an email than in a text or social media post. There is no limit to how long your email can be. If something needs a long sales pitch or description, email is a perfect fit.

Emails also don't disappear from the inbox. People can go back and read emails when they want to. It can be easier to find an old email from someone than an old social media post. You keep your presence in their inbox.

Have you ever tried calling clients or customers who never answer? It's so hard to get your message to them when their voice mailbox is full. But you still need to get information to them. Email can be another tool for you to get that information to them. You need to go through as many channels as you can to reach people, and email can help.

Another reason you should use email is that it's almost free to remarket to people once you have their email address. You can continue to send people emails over and over again without spending more money. With social media ads you have to continually pay to get your message in front of people. Now you do have to spend money on the email marketing software, but sending one email to a person is the same cost as sending 300 emails.

Lastly, if you "went for the kiss" and the person wasn't ready, you can continue to build the relationship with them through email. This will allow you to try again later. You can offer them something different to build more value. Also, staying in contact will help because when they are ready to buy, they think of you.

Show me the ways

There are two different ways to approach email marketing. The first way is to send an email blast. This is where you have a one-time message to get out. This is great if you launch a new product or video and you want to spread the word quickly. Specific promotions or flash sales are another reason to use an email blast. Another reason might be an event you want your customers to sign up for and participate in.

The second way to use email marketing is to send a sequence of emails over a period of time. This is great for multiple reasons. This is effective when someone opts in for your free lead magnet, for example. The first email would be sending the lead magnet and then following up to sell your product or get a sales appointment.

You use an email sequence to start building more of a relationship with people. Your email sequences should lead into the next stage of the dating strategy or to the goodnight kiss, aka a pitch for your product. Over a couple of days or weeks, you could be planting the seeds to get people to buy.

I could write books diving deeper into email marketing. However, this book is about learning the fundamentals. In the dating strategy earlier in the book, I outline where you should be using email, so you should have a great starting point.

Aim for the head

When breaking down the fundamentals of an email used in marketing, you first encounter the headline. The headline should be the main idea of your email. It should only hint at your main idea though. You want to spark people's interest so they are curious for more. You might use phrases such as: "What all the experts are saying..." or "Have I got a deal for you!"

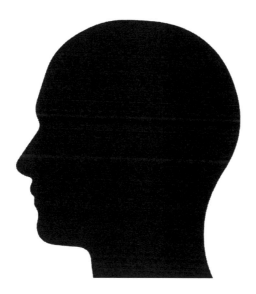

The goal of the headline is to stand out and grab people's attention. You want it to hint at what the email is about. Inboxes are crowded and you need to fight for the attention.

As I mentioned in my social media section, a great place to see headline examples is in beauty magazines. Also, try asking questions or using emojis in the headline. Try both long headlines and short ones. Try capitalizing just the first word of a sentence, or every word. Try asking a question or making a statement.

Again, it all comes back to... That's right: **FIO**!

Step 1: Try an advertisement (email) out.

Step 2: Look at the data.

Step 3: Make Adjustments.

Step 4: Repeat steps 1-3.

Are you sick of reading the word FIO? I'm not sorry. That is the mentality of a marketer and that is what you have to do in order to be successful.

Check out that body

Another fundamental is with the body of the email. Most emails you read are in paragraphs. That's how we learned to write in high school. That is NOT how you need to write marketing emails.

Every sentence should be on its own line. This makes it easier for people to read. It makes the email flow and helps more people read it because it looks like there is less to read. People's time is valuable, and they will find any excuse not to do something.

Here is an example of how your email format should look:

Hey (FirstName),

Sed ut perspiciatis unde omnis iste **natus error sit voluptatem accusantium** doloremque laudantium, totam rem aperiam.

Eaque ipsa quae ab illo inventore veritatis et quasi architecto beatae vitae dicta sunt explicabo.

Nemo **enim ipsam voluptatem** quia voluptas sit aspernatur aut odit aut fugit, sed quia consequuntur magni dolores eos qui ratione voluptatem sequi nesciunt.

Neque porro quisquam est, qui dolorem ipsum quia dolor sit amet, consectetur, adipisci velit, sed quia non numquam.

Eius modi tempora incidunt ut labore et dolore magnam aliquam quaerat voluptatem.

Quis autem vel eum iure reprehenderit qui in ea voluptate velit esse quam nihil molestiae consequatur, vel illum qui dolorem eum fugiat quo voluptas nulla pariatur?

I used Lorem Ipsum, which is a placeholder text for the email, but the initial look of the email shows it is easy to read. It isn't overwhelming to look at. A person can read it quickly.

That is the format for how you should write all of your marketing emails. This fundamental should also help with landing pages and social media. Make it as easy to read as possible. You can apply this to anywhere you write long pieces of information.

That's a bold move

Another thing you should do with your email copy is to bold the most important concepts. This will help the most important information stand out. If you need to add emphasis on a statement, bolding it will help.

Remember that some people will skim through what you write. Not everyone will take the time to go over everything. Bolding the most important parts will help someone get the most important information if they just skim through your email.

P.S.

What you can also do to help with the people that skim through your email (or landing page) is add a p.s. at the end. In the p.s., you just summarize the email so if someone jumps to the end without reading anything, they get the point of the email.

Don't ask people to multitask

Another recommendation is to have only one call-to-action. This is just like for landing pages. Always have just one purpose with your emails.

If you asked people to sign up for something AND follow you on social media AND reply if they have any questions, you will get nothing. Give them one thing to do per email and two to three places to do it (just like with landing pages).

Treat everyone like grandma

Another quick fundamental with emails that people don't think about is the font of the email. If you use small font, it will be harder to read.

Think about it. If someone reads their email on their smartphone, small font is even smaller. I like to use at least 16 point font in all of my emails so that even a grandma could read it.

This is why

At the beginning of my book I said marketing fundamentals build off each other. Well here is an example of the reason I don't want people jumping around in this book. What I said about the email copy applies to landing pages and social media copy as well.

They are very similar. Don't write big long paragraphs. Use a bigger font. Make it easy to read. Have one call-to-action in multiple places.

You can find success with email marketing if you do it right. It takes time and a lot of skill. But now you have a place to start.

Remember that not all businesses need to rely on email marketing. Just like not all businesses need to be on Facebook or Twitter. What you need to do is evaluate if and how different platforms fit with your business. Once you do, then you get to work on FIO.

Recap of email fundamentals:

- Test everything
- Headlines should spark interest in the email
- Make your email body easy to read
- Use bigger font size
- Include only one CTA, but multiple places to act

Chapter 8

SMS/BOTS the shiny new toys

New tools and software are popping up every day it seems. They help bring in better ways to reach and connect with people. These tools are fun and can make marketing a million times easier.

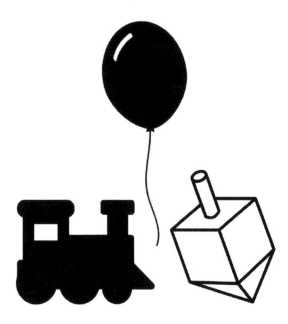

As a marketer, you should be staying up to date on platforms you are currently using, as well as keeping an eye on what's new. Keeping up to date will help because you never know what could change your business for the better. Knowing what is out there will help you continually improve your strategy.

I believe that no matter what tool you are using, you must stick to the basics and fundamentals. As new tools come out, you'll be tempted to jump in and use everything right away. But you don't need to use everything that's new. It's easy with new tools to skip steps and make mistakes. Then you may repeat what happened with email marketing, and the effectiveness decreases.

Another reason you shouldn't just use everything that is new is that not everything is right for your business. For example, not every business should be using Google AdWords. Google AdWords is great for businesses whose product is something that people search for. If your business isn't something people typically search for then that means your audience isn't there.

Those kind of business should be focusing on a platform like Facebook because it's a great at getting in front of people who aren't looking for your product but need it. You need to be able to take a look at what you want to accomplish and find the best way to get there.

Some new and exciting marketing tools are SMS Marketing and BOT Marketing. SMS stands for Short Message Service. Most know this as text message marketing. BOT marketing is very similar, but I'll explain SMS Marketing first.

My favorite

Now, I love SMS marketing. It isn't necessarily new, but it is becoming cheaper and easier to use. The software company I worked for was an SMS marketing platform. I see so much power in texting if it is done right.

I can tell you about some amazing case studies in SMS marketing. With one message I helped a company make over $75,000 on Black Friday. They quadrupled their sales from the year before. Another company grew revenue by 18% in one month by adding one of my SMS marketing strategies. I helped a small retail store that had only been open a few months bring in $5,000 in one weekend by sending one text message to a list of about 200 people.

The point is, texting is a powerful tool. Staying in touch all year long is hard. Communication is difficult for any business and is something that most companies need to improve.

Your goal with marketing is to build relationships and trust. Texting can be non-imposing and non-threatening.

The following are just a few benefits of SMS marketing:

- Sending simple text messages can help you nurture and connect with your clients.
- It can help you warm up your customers and leads to buying.
- You can easily stay in contact with potential customers all year round.
- It allows you to follow up with clients in order to upsell.
- You are able to ask for referrals and message the referrals you receive.

- It allows you to remind people about appointments.

Look at the numbers

What makes texting so effective though? Texts have around a 90%-98% open rate. That number varies from business to business. Some studies will say 98%, while others will say 92%. Yours might be different, but generally text open rates are extremely high.

SMS marketing now is similar to email marketing 10 years ago. It provides high open rates and success without requiring extensive skill. Over time, email was diluted with bad marketing, and now there are spam folders and promotion folders hurting your open rates.

SMS marketing isn't there quite yet. I predict that very soon cell phone providers will start having spam and promotion folders just like they do for email. As this happens, the open rates for text messages will decrease and become less effective, unfortunately. But currently, it can be a highly effective marketing tool.

The same but different

SMS marketing is different from email marketing. Yet marketers will make the mistake of trying to use it the same way. This principle can be applied to any type of marketing: use the tool the way the tool was meant to be used. Nails and screws are very similar and can sometimes be switched in and out easily for the same job, but don't try and hammer a screw or drill in a nail.

Here are some examples of the differences between texts and emails. Text messages need to be around 160 characters. You have to be able to fit your message into a small amount of space. Emails can be much longer, so you can give more details and information.

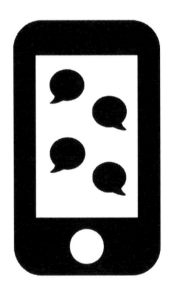

Now I could write a whole book on SMS marketing. I actually have written a short one on different SMS strategies that I used as a lead magnet in the past. But again, this book is for fundamentals. I want to show you how powerful SMS marketing can be.

Feel the power

Just think about it, the average American checks his or her phone roughly 150 times a day. It seems everyone has a cell phone. Most people prefer to text rather than talk on the phone.

I personally never answer a phone call unless I have the contact's info saved. Even when I know who is calling, most of the time I let it go to voicemail. Texting is easier.

Learn from others' mistakes

SMS marketing can be very simple. You are trying to either get a quick piece of information to someone or you are trying to start a conversation with a person.

SMS marketing should be called conversational marketing. A mistake people make when using SMS marketing is that they try and do too much with a single text message. Remember, you should never try to get cold customers or leads to buy over a text message.

I have seen this happen with a business owner using an SMS platform. He was a business coach. I was helping him with contacting old leads that had gone cold. His goal was to reach out and see if they had a moment to talk on the phone. I crafted his message to be very simple: introducing himself again and asking them how their business was doing. That was it. He could then strike up a conversation without the text coming on too strong.

The goal was to get a conversation going. After he got a person started in a conversation, he would set up an appointment to get him or her on a call for a FREE strategy session. This way he would start warming up these cold leads.

The response was amazing. He had a list of around 400 people. Within 15 minutes, he had over 40% of the leads responding. That's around 160ish leads.

If he had tried to call all the leads it would have taken him three or four weeks. Instead, he set up appointments for the next few weeks. To make a long story short, he made a lot of money off those old leads. The most important part of this is that he didn't have to waste time just trying to get in contact with them.

The next time he tried this, he didn't do it the same way. He tried to do it himself, and he ended up writing a five-page text (800 characters). He started by introducing himself, asking how their business was doing, asking if they had thought more about the coaching, seeing when there was a time to talk, and asking what their interest level was in coaching. All of this in one text message!

He had a response rate of less than 5% total. He didn't make any sales. In his process, he ruined the relationship with most of those old leads. He came across too strongly to an audience that wasn't warmed up. It was like going up to an ex or someone he had been on one date with a few months ago and trying to kiss them without warning.

This is a great example of how the little things matter with marketing. The fundamentals matter. If you understand how a tool is supposed to be used, you will be more successful.

This will help when you are looking into new marketing tools. If you learn how to use marketing tools properly, when you try a new tool you'll have much more success.

You have to be careful

SMS marketing can also be easily abused. You must be very careful to only send promotional texts to people who have opted in. The best thing to do is stay up-to-date on the laws and regulations regarding text marketing, and they are constantly changing. A quick Google search will help you get started in the right direction.

If you do it right, SMS can be your best friend. With the high open rates it has, asking for referrals and surveys can be wildly successful. Contacting those precious leads as soon as you generate them will help increase conversions and get you more sales pitches. Also, you can get more people to actually show up for appointments. SMS Marketing is awesome!

Robots are taking over the world

I will also include BOTS in this chapter, as they are very similar to SMS marketing. BOTS are chat boxes you see when you go to a website. They'll usually ask you how you're doing or if there is anything they can do for you. They are essentially a virtual store manager.

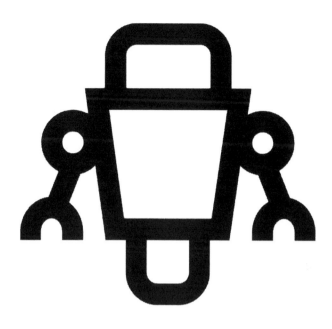

You can also build out BOTS on some of the major social media platforms. This is awesome! What a better way to build relationships with people than to start having a conversation with them right from your social media or website!

The goal should mostly be to start conversations. I say mostly because there are occasions to use them differently. BOTS are also still very new, and there will be changes with them over the next few years.

Using BOTS to get a conversation going will help you find out if a person really is interested in your products or services, or if he or she is just looking around. You can use them to see if they are your ideal client or not. Let me explain.

Just Like A Physical Store

First, your website is like your digital store and your landing pages are like booths. Imagine you walk into a clothing store. There are employees in stores who will ask you if there is anything you need as soon as you walk in. The same is true for a booth at an expo or convention.

Most of the time, the employee will ask, "Is there anything you need?" or "Let me know if you have any questions." These are terrible questions to ask. They are too broad. They kill any chance of starting a conversation.

It would be better if the employee asked something like, "Are you just looking around or is there something specific you're looking for?" This is great because it is Identifying if this person is really interested and if the employee should spend more time with them.

Now compare this to using a BOT on your site. This is how you should be using your BOT on your website or landing page. You should be asking something like, "Are you [your ideal client]?" If they say yes, you know this is the right kind of client and you should spend more time with them. If they answer no, then great! The reason that is great is that now you don't have to waste time with them.

If they say yes, then you can use follow-up questions. Dig deeper, and try to determine if they are experiencing some of the pain points you help with. Then ask them what brought them to your website or landing page. Ask them if they know about your product.

All of this will lead to you pointing them in the direction of your product or getting on a sales call. Just like in the dating cycle, you need to build that relationship first.

With BOTS that are built correctly, you can start that relationship as soon as a person visits your landing page or website. It's just as if they walked into a physical store.

Automatic or manual?

If you could chat with every single person who came to your landing page or website, it would be very time-consuming. You have more important things to do than to ask people the same questions over and over again. And people will come to your website when you aren't available.

If you want to make this a smooth process, you build the BOT to automatically ask all the initial questions for you. When I say automatically, I don't mean you'll never have to talk to people or message them yourself. But you can have BOTS built out so they ask the first set of qualifying questions. This is very efficient as you don't have to ask them yourself.

You can now build these BOTS without even knowing how to code. There are plenty of software programs that will make it easy and simple for you. With it built out to automatically ask the questions, you won't have to message back every person who comes to your website or landing page.

This way, once the data generated from the questions have verified they are the right kind of client, you can then take over at the right time. Send them to your scheduling software. Ask them when they are available to talk. Push them to a product, etc.

Sometimes saying no is the best choice

The objective of this chapter is to help you understand some of the lesser-known tools available. Also, you should understand that there are new tools continually being introduced. Here is the thing: you don't have to say yes to all of them.

What is the difference between little kids and professionals playing soccer? Obviously, several things. The main difference is that the kids are like watching a herd of cats chasing a ball of yarn. Wherever the ball goes, everyone runs to it. Marketers do this with marketing tools.

On the other hand, professionals all know their roles. They stick to their positions. They work together and are disciplined to wait. They stick to the fundamentals. You need to be like this with your marketing, especially when it comes to the different tools and software available.

As you look at all the tools available, it's easy to get caught up in the features of the tool. But you don't always need those features. You'll waste time trying to fit features into your marketing. Instead, find the features to make your marketing work the best.

You need to FIO over and over again. This is how you get in the marketing mindset. This is how you will become successful in marketing.

Chapter 9

Data

I've explained the fundamentals of marketing and some different marketing tools. Now you should be able to go into any marketing situation and start with a foundation that can lead to success. But what does success mean in marketing?

You will never convert 100% of anything in marketing. You'll never convert 100% of the people who have come to your landing page to opt-in, even for free lead magnets. Successful conversion rates can look small compared to what we generally think is successful.

Knowing why something is or isn't converting is one of the hardest parts of being a marketer. The reason it's so hard is that there are so many moving parts.

You can work super hard on your strategy and everything in it, and then it doesn't convert people into sales. The worst part is you might not even know what's going wrong.

What you need to look at is the data: Step 2 of FIO.

Data Dyslexia

Data is nothing if you don't know how to read it. It can be compared to expecting to gain results by buying a self-help book. It won't help you just to have it. You need to read the book and apply what you learn.

This is how you need to look at your data. Data is only as valuable as what you get out of it. You need to be able to read it and understand the story it's telling.

People sometimes get the idea that graphs equal data. This is false. Data is not having a ton of graphs. Graphs are just a tool to make reading the data easier.

Not every strategy works. I've had plenty of ads and strategies fall flat on their faces. You will have lots of failures. You won't have to take my word for it. Once you start running campaigns and strategies, you will see failures too. But you can take those failures and learn from them through understanding your data. You can turn those failures into successes. You'll be able to continually improve as a marketer.

Break it down for me

I'm going to dive into step 2 of FIO. Look at the data. If you know what the data is telling you, you will know where to make adjustments.

Now there are standard results in every platform and step in the strategy to measure with. The numbers I will give you are what I use to measure success. But it's different for every business or industry.

Some industries might have a higher email open rate than others. Or their social media engagement rates are higher than another industries. For example, a warm audience or list will always outperform a cold audience or list.

Always give credence to your own data rather than others'. Yours is the data you can trust and build upon. If you don't have a lot of your own data yet, you can look up your industry's results. This will give you specifics and a good idea of where you want to be.

In marketing, we call these numbers Key Performance Indicators or KPI's. KPI's help you know what is working and what isn't. Every platform and industry have different KPI's. Let me give you the ones I look at and then you can build upon that in the future.

Social Media

Let's take a look at social media first. For **organic social media** posts, I like seeing 3% engagement. What that means is 3% of anyone who has seen the post engaged with it by liking, commenting, sharing, or performing any other action.

If you are getting lower engagement than that, here are some changes you can make:

1. Use higher quality pictures

2. Ask people to engage and tell them why they should
3. Try switching between videos and pictures

As you make posts that get higher engagement, keep track of what you did to get those results. Always analyze what is working and what isn't. Look at your competition and see what kind of posts are getting higher engagement and try to figure out why.

For **social media ads,** your CTR or Click-Through Rate is something to monitor when running ads. CTR is the percent of people who saw the ad, clicked on the ad, and took action. This KPI varies greatly depending on whether you have a cold audience or a warm audience.

Cold audiences are people who don't know you and are meeting you for the first time. Warm audiences are people with whom you have already built trust. They know who you are. You should expect a higher CTR with a warm audience.

Your CTR also depends on what platform you are using. To figure out what your benchmark CTR should be, Google it. Look up the average CTR for your industry. For example, "What is the average click-through rate for the fitness industry on Pinterest?" This is one way you can find and set a standard for your ads.

Another KPI for ads that is similar to CTR is your CPC (Cost per Click). Again, to find what your industry cost per click should be, Google it. If you are seeing higher than normal CPC, or if your CPC is rising it means your ads needs adjustments.

If your ads are not working, following are some things to adjust. This is the order in which I make adjustments:

1. Adjust the image/video
2. Adjust the headline
3. Adjust the copy
4. Look at the audience and make sure you are targeting the right type of people

Landing Pages

I measure landing pages (where you send people) just like I do the ads. With a warm audience, I like to have a 20 - 40% opt-in success rate as a starting point. For a cold audience which will always have a lower success rate, I start around 10 - 20%.

These numbers are different if you are giving something for free or if you are selling a low-cost item. If you are selling a low-cost item, you are going to see lower results than something that's free. So your standard to measure should be lower as well.

When you're not seeing the results you like, here are some changes to make:

1. Make sure you have clear benefit statements, social proof, and you are establishing yourself as an authority
2. Make changes to the copy
3. Switch between long page and short page
4. Change the colors of the buttons
5. Change out the images

Email

Email open rates should be between 20-30%. Click-through rates should be around 3-8%. If you are seeing lower open rates, your subject line isn't very good. If your click-through rates are low, then your copy isn't very good, and that's where you need to make changes.

Changes to make are:

1. Open rates are down = change the subject line
2. Clicks are down = change the copy

Email is simpler to measure results and look at the data for than some of the other tools available.

SMS

Data for SMS is still so new and difficult to gauge.

1. I rely on about a 90-98% open rate.
2. When I can include a link that can track clicks, I aim for a 20% click-through rate.
3. When I'm asking for responses, I aim for about a 30% response rate.

Changes to make are:

1. Change the copy
2. Make sure you only have one call to action
3. Ask a simpler question

BOTS

With BOTS we have the same issue as with SMS marketing. It is still so new that data is hard to determine. Look at your BOTS and compare the percent of people who engage with them to how many people come to your landing page. I like to have a 20% BOT engagement rate.

Changes to make are:

1. Change the copy
2. Make sure you only have one call to action
3. Ask a simpler question

The Key

With all your marketing, everything takes time. A mistake every marketer can easily make is to become discouraged when something doesn't work right away. Running a Facebook ad for one day and not getting a single lead doesn't mean the ad is ineffective.

I like to base all these numbers on about 100-500 people, depending on my budget. This will give you a much better idea than 10 people. The more traffic or people you have, the better your data will reflect. You might get your first person to your landing page to convert, and then the next 99 don't. Be patient with your funnels and strategies.

This exact situation happened to me when running ads for a client. I was running ads for an eCommerce store. The very first click became a sale. I was super pumped and thought that the ad would just continue to roll. BOY WAS I WRONG. That ad ended up being terrible.

You need to take your time. The first 80 people might not buy or opt-in, but the next 20 might. If you get discouraged quickly and start changing things before you've given it enough time, you'll never know the true results.

Chapter 10

The Conclusion

We have come to the end of the book. Congratulations! You are now one step closer to becoming a digital marketing baller. You should feel confident that you can now get started in digital marketing for your business.

After reading this book, you should have an understanding of the dating strategy. You should also have an understanding of the fundamentals in every step of marketing. And you should also have an understanding of FIO.

For finishing this book, I applaud you. Finishing anything, no matter how small, is a win. Most people make plans and have dreams but never see them all the way through.

I believe the only time we ever fail is when we give up. There are times where the right move is to move on after putting in a solid effort. There will be times where you need to move on from a landing page that just won't get the job done.

You're not a failure if something doesn't work. Welcome to life! Most things don't work out. But you fail if you just give up because something is hard. This is the attitude you need to have with marketing, and with life in general.

My inspiration

I want to share with you a story that really impacted my life and inspired the title of this book.

When I was in school, I took a web development class. It was not my favorite subject, but I really liked the teacher so it wasn't too bad. He was awesome! He wasn't like most professors. He had real life experience and knew his stuff.

On the last day of class, he asked us a question, "Who is the best player in the NBA?" Some people said Lebron James, while others said Michael Jordan, and a couple people said Steph Curry. Then my teacher asked, "What do all these guys have in common?"

He went on to explain, "All of these guys are Ballers. They are considered the best at what they do. Whatever your profession is, you need to be the best at what you do. You need to be The Baller. Whenever someone asks, 'Who is good at this?' your goal should be that your name is the name that is brought up."

I came away from that class determined that no matter what I did with work or in my personal life, that would be my goal. To be The Baller. That is why I named this book *Becoming a Digital Baller the Playbook*. That's the goal. To be The Baller of digital marketing.

I want to help others with that as well. I want you to become The Baller of coaching, personal training, real estate, e-commerce, modeling, speaking, being a mechanic, or whatever your business is. And as you become a Digital Marketing Baller, you will be on your way to reaching your goals as a business owner.

Remember it will be hard. You will want to quit when you get stuck, but you can get through it!

Don't forget to get your FREE trainings mentioned throughout the book here: www.thedigitalballer.com/amazon

Now go become a Digital Baller.

ABOUT THE AUTHOR

Connor Wright began his path in digital marketing as he majored in social media marketing in college. He started out helping friends and family with their social media.

He quickly got a job as the Director of Marketing for an SMS marketing software company. He helped double their growth in less than a year and helped clients generate millions of dollars through SMS marketing, he then left and joined a digital agency.

While at this agency he has generated tens of millions of dollars in almost every industry and every aspect of digital marketing (Social media, Email, SMS, Automation, & Digital Ads).

His goal is to one day be considered the G.O.A.T. of Digital Marketing.

Made in the USA
San Bernardino, CA
10 September 2019